HAL•LEONARD INSTRUMENTAL PLAY-ALONG

AUDIO ACCESS INCLUDED

PLAYBACK+
Speed • Pitch • Balance • Loop

HORN

Disney

Beauty AND THE Beast

T0086638

To access audio visit:
www.halleonard.com/mylibrary

Enter Code
5002-0281-6374-5214

ISBN 978-1-4950-9614-3

Motion Picture Artwork, TM & Copyright
© 2017 Disney Enterprises, Inc.

**Wonderland Music Company, Inc.
Walt Disney Music Company**

DISTRIBUTED BY

HAL•LEONARD®
7777 W. BLUEMOUND RD. P.O. BOX 13819 MILWAUKEE, WI 53213

In Australia Contact:
Hal Leonard Australia Pty. Ltd.
4 Lentara Court
Cheltenham, Victoria, 3192 Australia
Email: ausadmin@halleonard.com.au

Visit Hal Leonard Online at
www.halleonard.com

ARIA

HORN

Music by ALAN MENKEN
Lyrics by TIM RICE

Moderately, getting faster throughout

BE OUR GUEST

Horn

Music by ALAN MENKEN
Lyrics by HOWARD ASHMAN

BEAUTY AND THE BEAST

HORN

Music by ALAN MENKEN
Lyrics by HOWARD ASHMAN

BELLE

Horn

Music by ALAN MENKEN
Lyrics by HOWARD ASHMAN

DAYS IN THE SUN

HORN

Music by ALAN MENKEN
Lyrics by TIM RICE

EVERMORE

HORN

Music by ALAN MENKEN
Lyrics by TIM RICE

GASTON

HORN

Music by ALAN MENKEN
Lyrics by HOWARD ASHMAN

HOW DOES A MOMENT LAST FOREVER

HORN

Music by ALAN MENKEN
Lyrics by TIM RICE

THE MOB SONG

Horn

Music by ALAN MENKEN
Lyrics by HOWARD ASHMAN

SOMETHING THERE

HORN

Music by ALAN MENKEN
Lyrics by HOWARD ASHMAN